# What A Wonderful World Around Us

## Keep your eyes on what is around you

### Janet Wolfe

# WHAT A WONDERFUL WORLD AROUND US

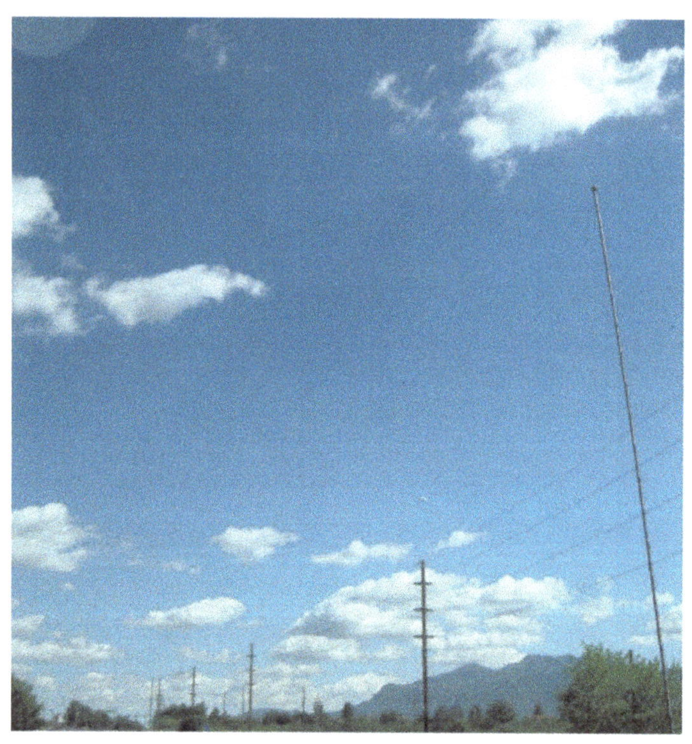

## JANET WOLFE

Book Films Media
+1 (725) 238-6534
www.bookfilmsmedia.com

# The Canadian Geese are heading South. Here they have landed at Tamarack Lake in Lakeview, Michigan.

"…Oh that I had wings like a (Canadian Goose)! For then would I fly away, and be at rest."

Psalm 55:6

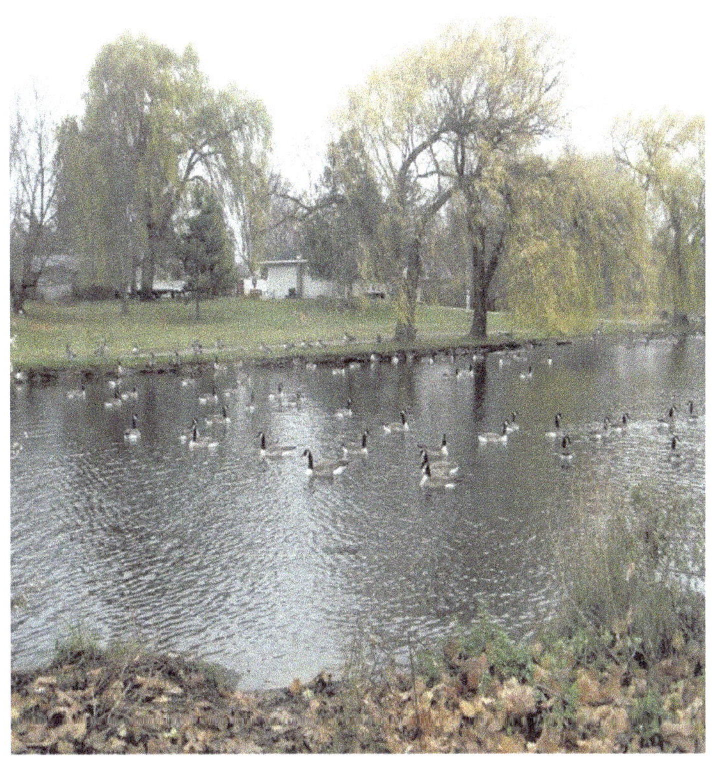

# The Rocks and Mesquite Trees along I10 heading toward Bisbee, Arizona.

---

"For from the top of the rocks I see him, and from the hills I behold him…"

Numbers 23:9

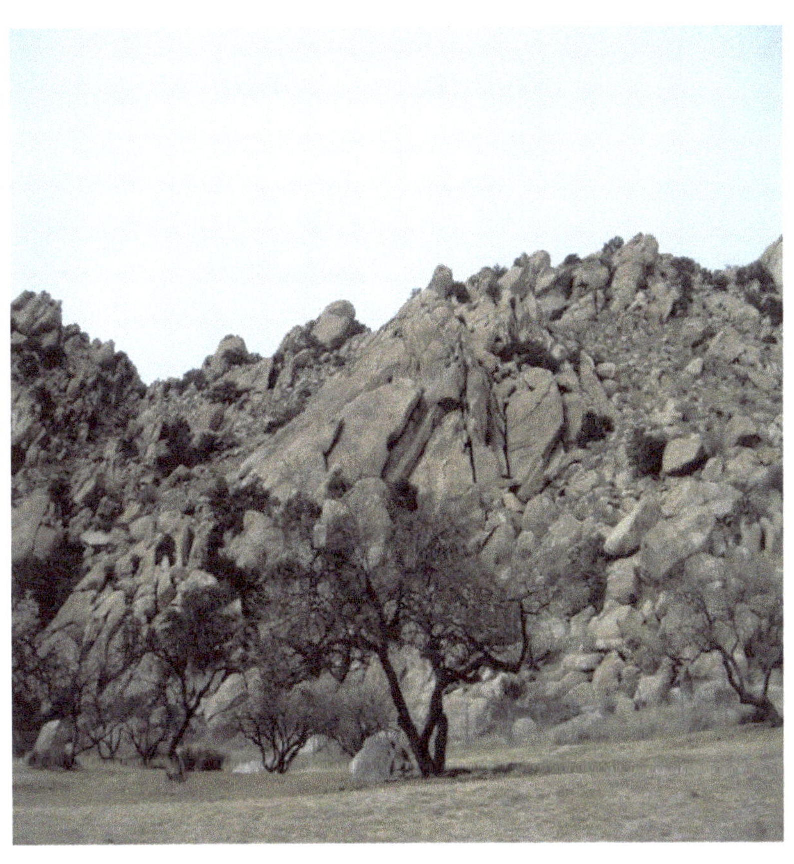

# Amazing Soil and Rock colors from the minerals found therein Bisbee, Arizona.

---

"…and the earth did quake, and the rocks rent…"

Matthew 27:51

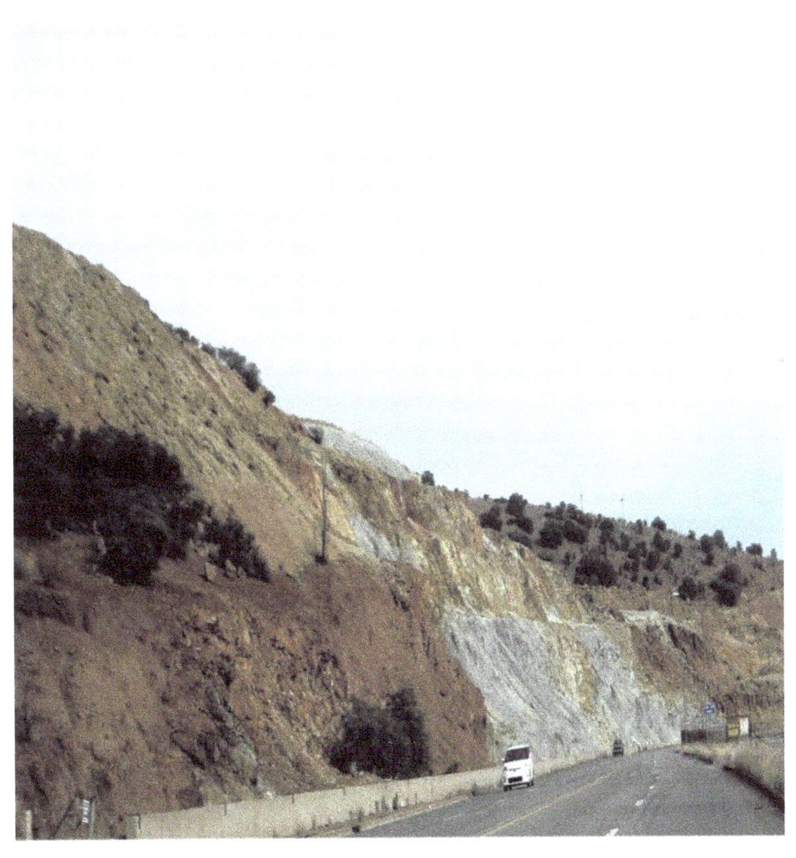

# The Mariachi Dancers at Pancho Villa Days in Columbus, Mexico.

"Praise Him with the timbrel and dance…"

Psalm 150:3

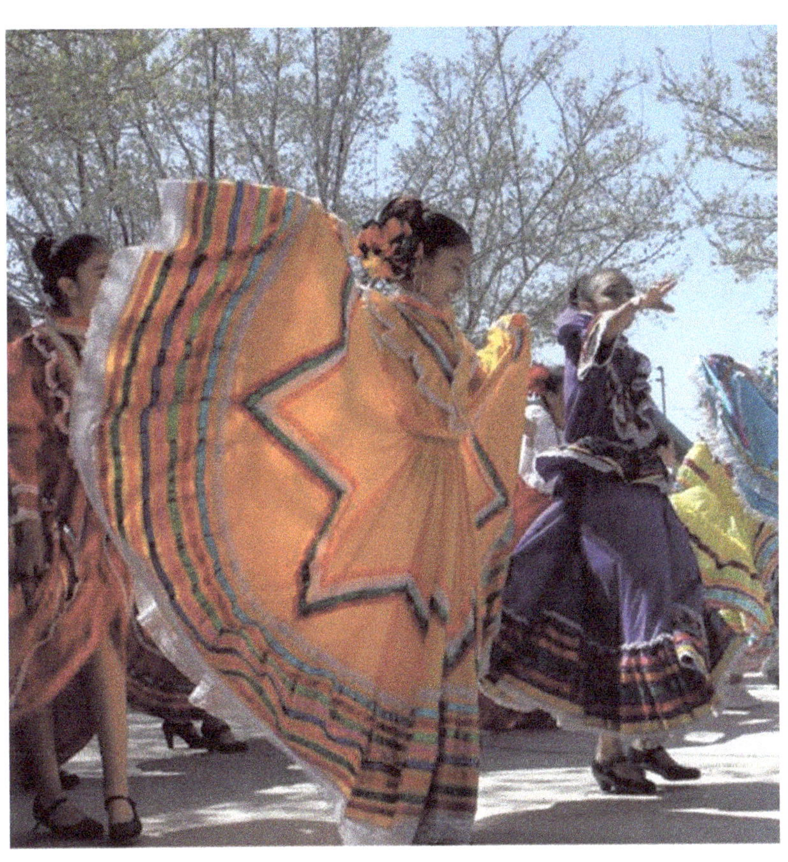

# The Mariachi's from Mexico really know how to dance at Pancho Villa Days in Columbus, New Mexico!

---

"Thou hast turned for me my mourning into dancing..."

Psalm 30:10

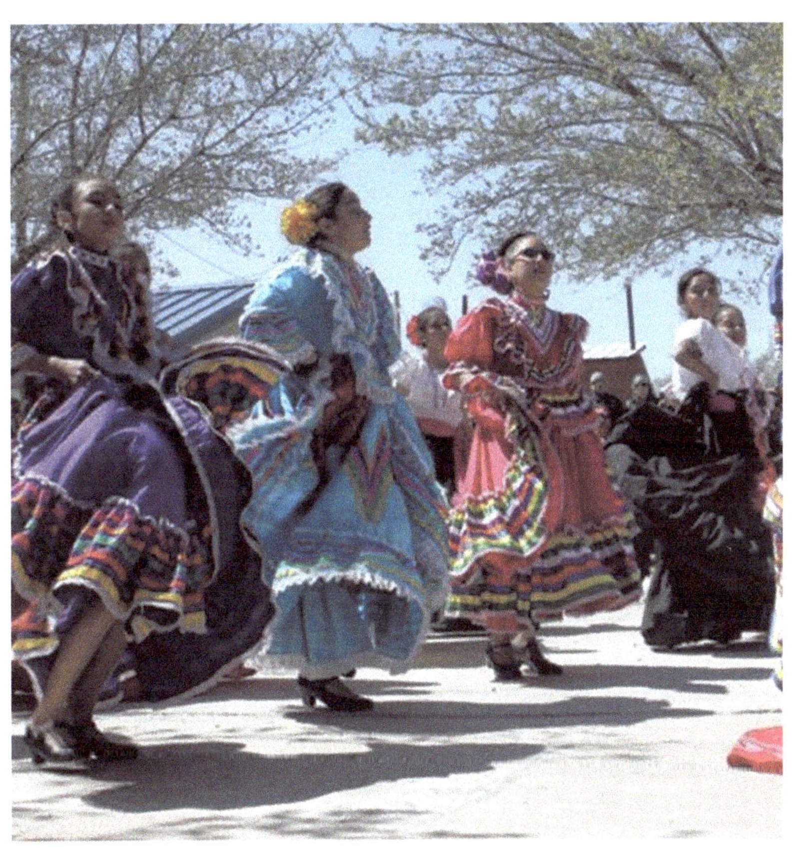

# And the Ladies are joined by the Gentlemen!

"And David danced before the Lord with all His might"

II Samuel 6:14

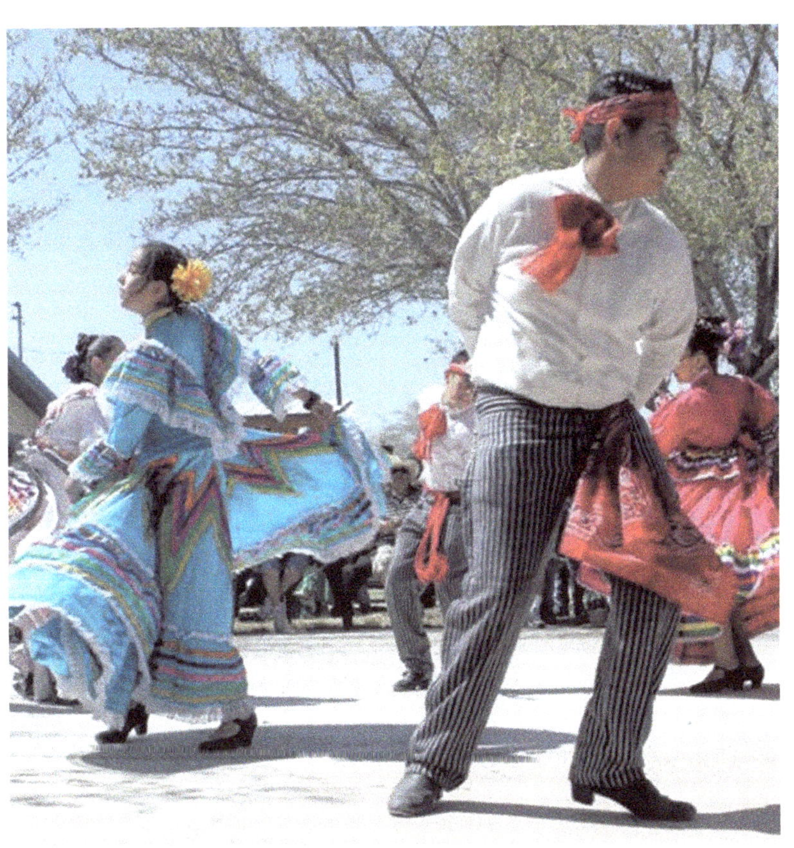

# Mariachi Dancers provide great entertainment at many functions throughout the Southwest.

---

"Sing, O heavens; and be joyful, O earth, and break forth into singing, O mountains; for the Lord hath comforted His people..."

Isaiah 49:13

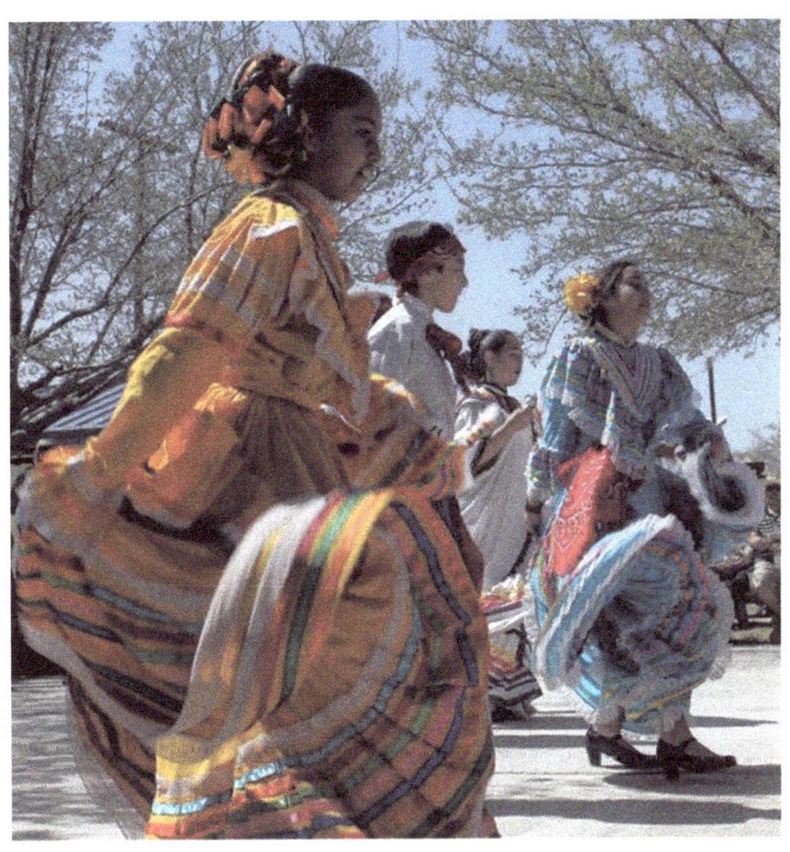

# Open Pit Mining was one part of the rapid growth of Bisbee, Arizona.

---

"In all labour there is profit…"

Proverbs 14:23

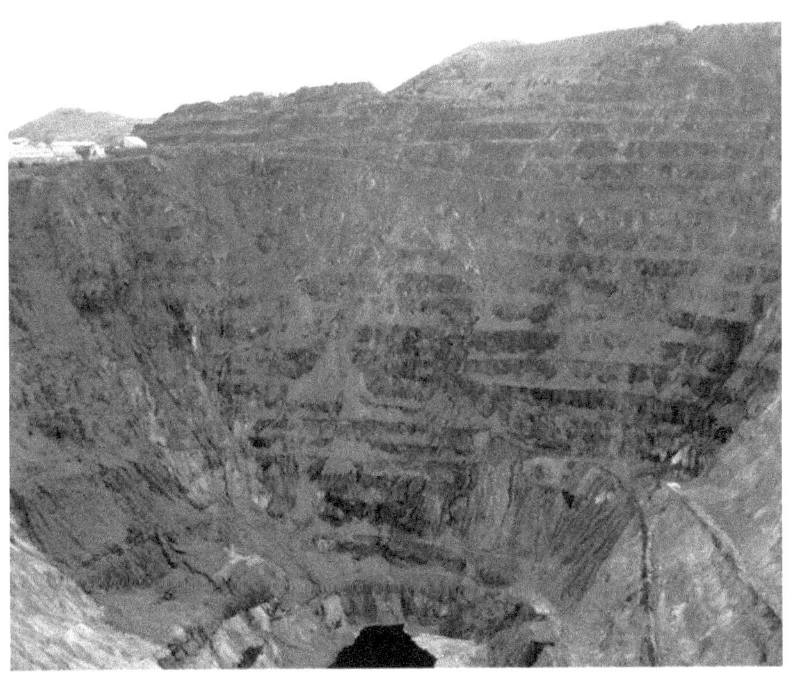

# The open Pit is very deep;
# here is the bottom.

---

"…for the Spirit searcheth all things, yea, the deep Things of God."

I Corinthians 2:10

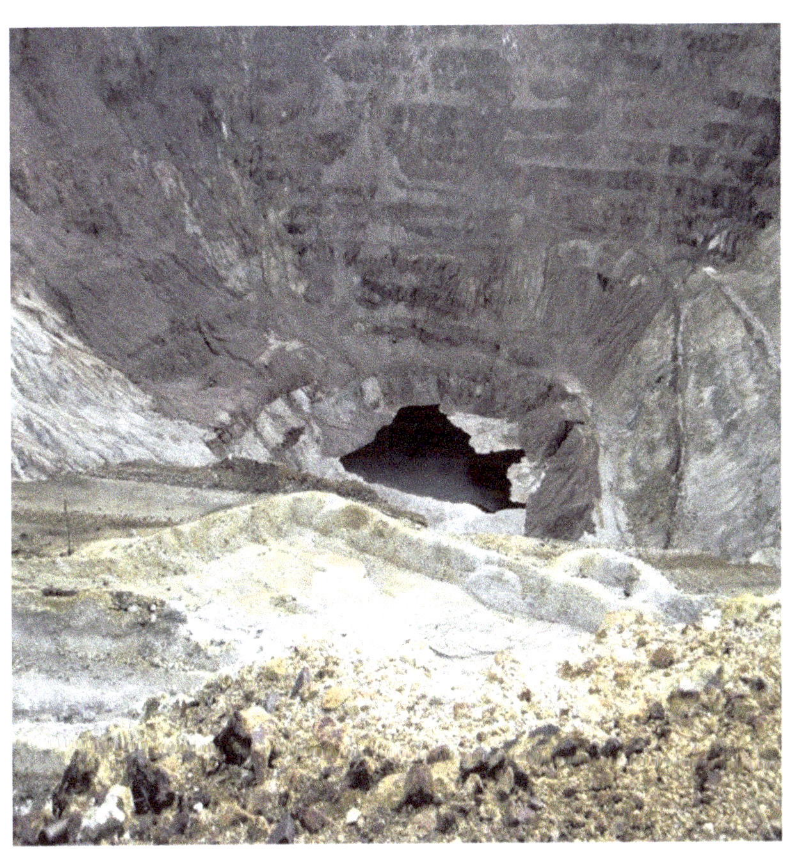

# There is a great winding pathway to reach the bottom of the Pit.

---

"That Christ may dwell in your hearts by faith; that ye, being rooted and grounded in love, May be able to Comprehend with all saints what is the breadth, and Length, and depth, and height; And to know the love Of Christ, which passeth knowledge, that ye might be Filled with all the fullness of God."

Ephesians 3:17-19

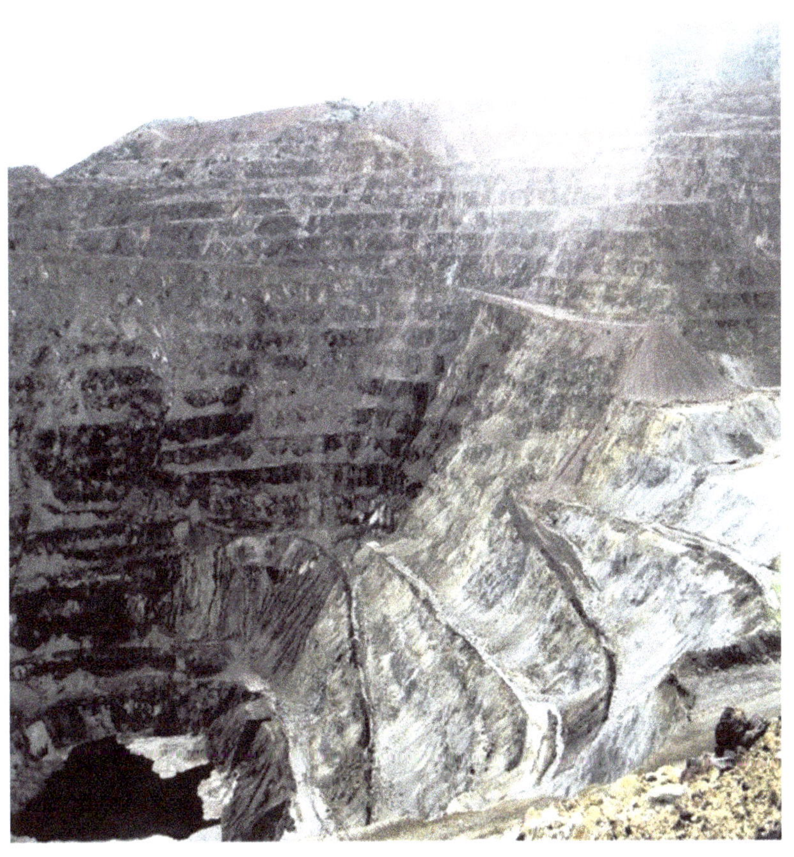

The walls of the Pit
tell a great story
as to what type of mineral
was found at each level of the Mine.

---

"He is the Rock; His work is perfect for all His ways
are judgment: a God of truth and without iniquity, just and right is He."

Deuteronomy 32:4

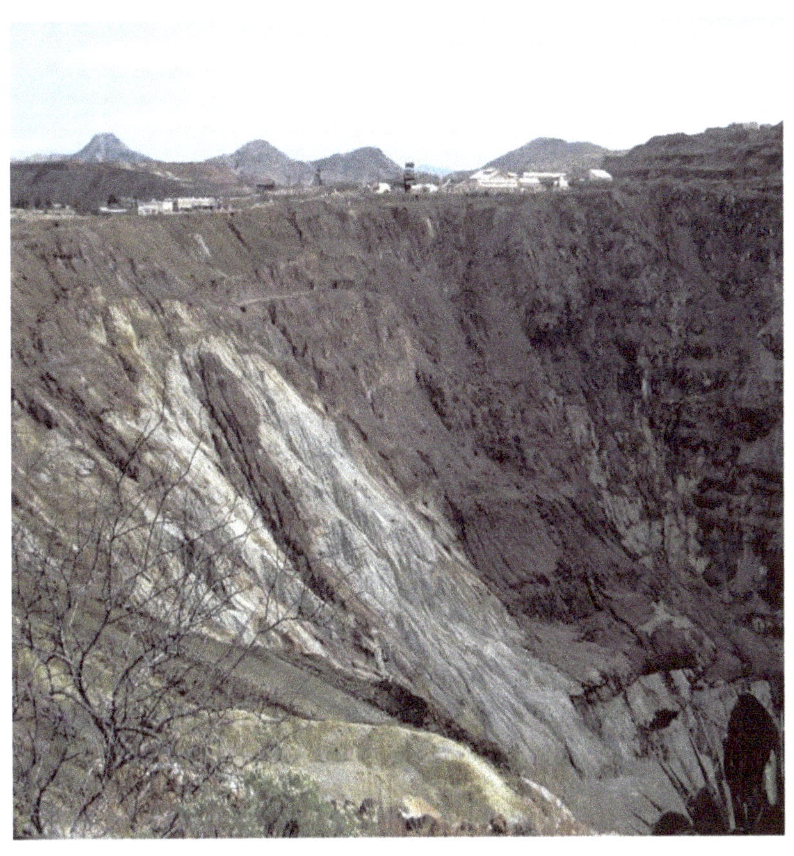

One way to get your attention
is to make a big point directly aimed at
you!
This is the canon
at Fort Bayard, New Mexico,
during Ft. Bayard Celebration.

---

"My son, attend to My words; incline thine ear unto my sayings."

Proverbs 4:20

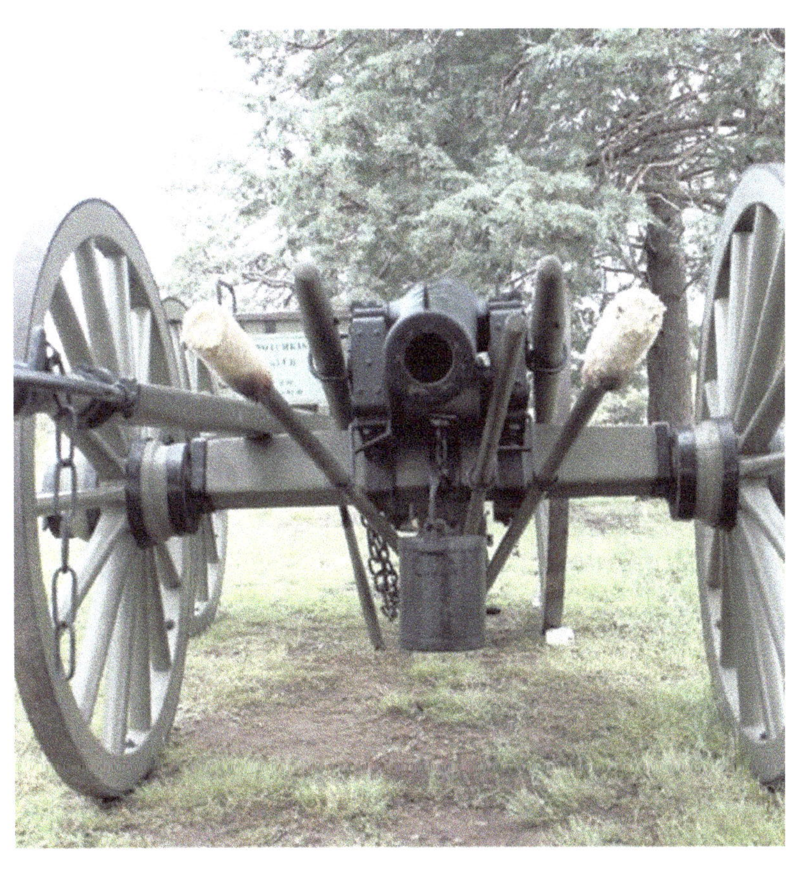

Even children can make Adobe Bricks,
as seen in this photo taken
at the Ft. Bayard Days Celebration,
at Ft. Bayard, New Mexico.

---

"Even a child is known by his doings,
whether his work be pure, and whether it be right."

Proverbs 20:11

"Train up a child in the way he should go:
and when he is old, he will not depart from it."

Proverbs 22:6

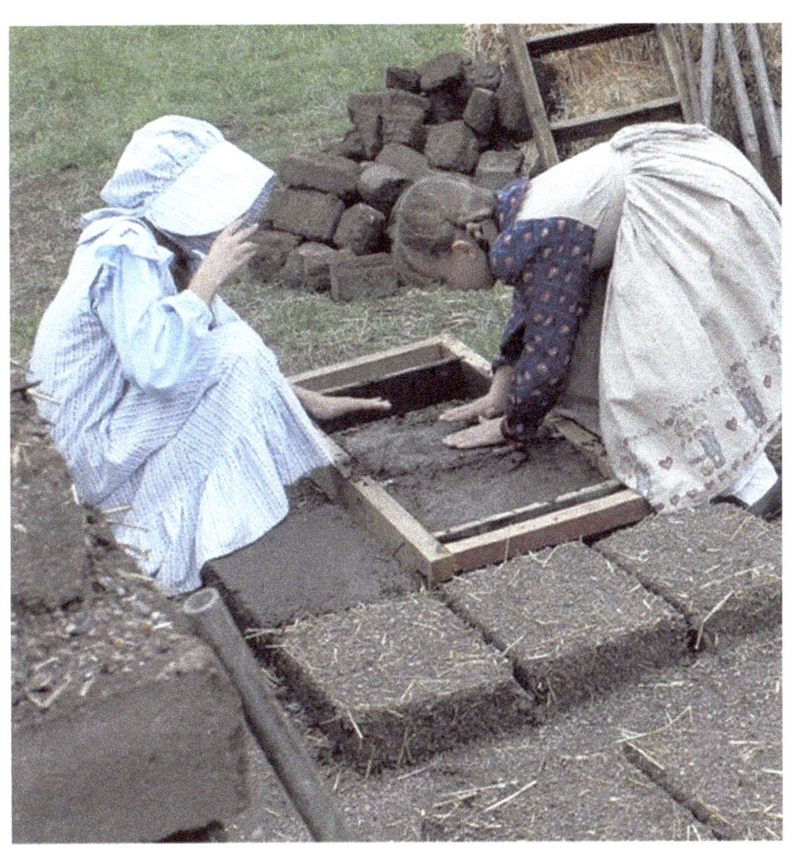

The Ft. Bayard Cemetery
is very impressive,
the men and women who are buried here
will long be remembered
for their contribution to our Country
in both times of War and times of peace.

---

"Therefore, my brethren dearly beloved and longed for, my joy and
crown, so stand fast in the Lord…"

Philippians 4:1

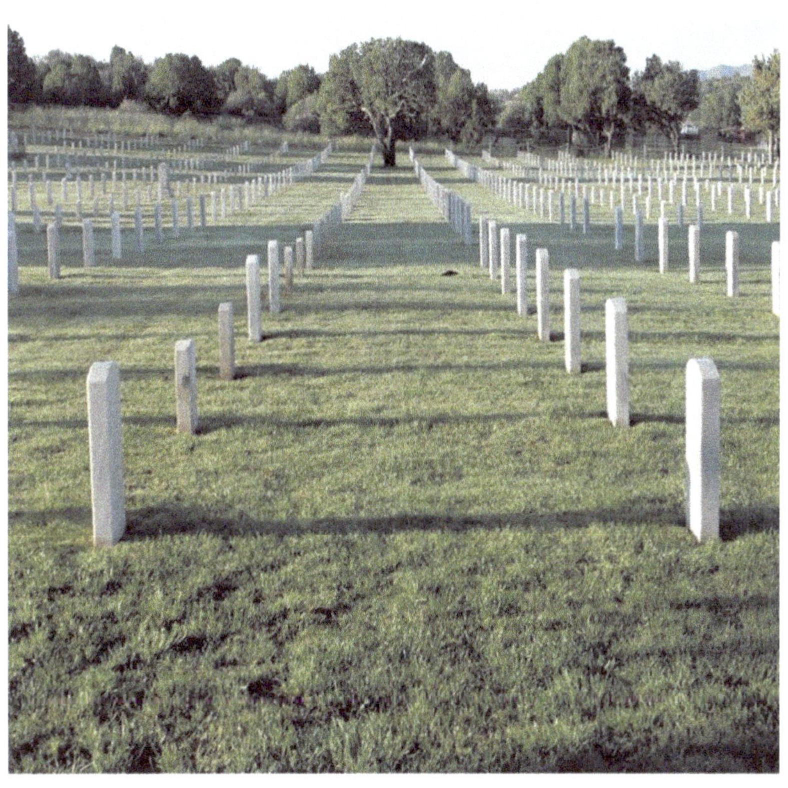

In order to walk one block over,
this is how it is done in Bisbee, Arizona.
The town is built in steep mountains –
that's where mining could be done.

---

"For as the heavens are higher than the earth, so are My ways higher
than your ways, and My thoughts than your thoughts."

Isaiah 55:9

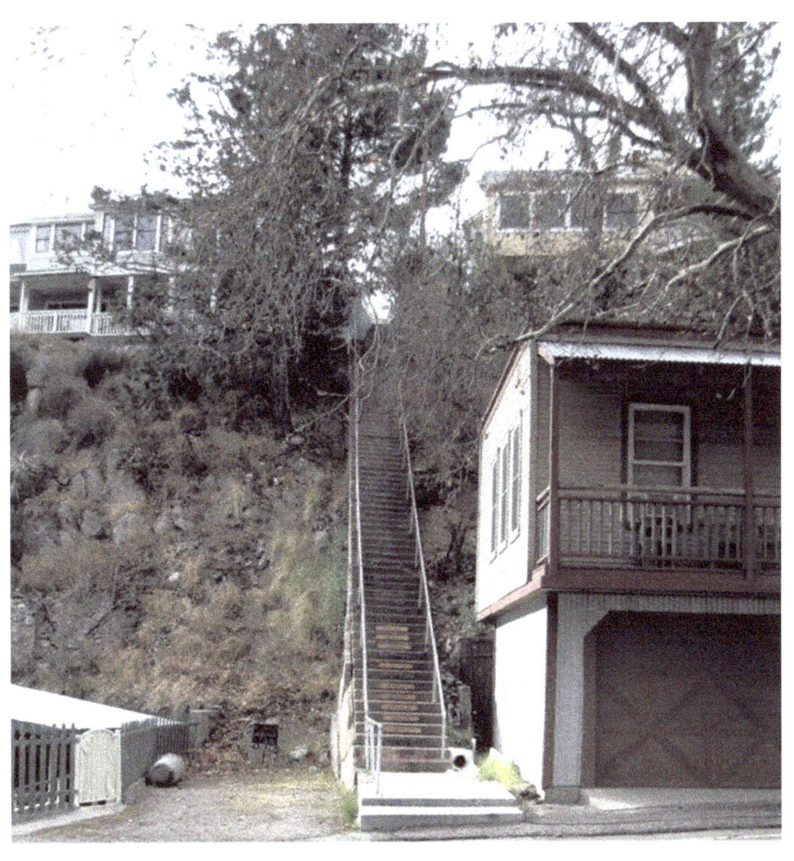

At Pony Hills, north of Deming,
New Mexico, there are stories to be read.
These are the Petroglyphs, where Native
Americans told of their exploits.

---

"Forasmuch as ye are manifestly declared to be the epistle of Christ
ministered by us, written not with ink, but with the Spirit of the living
God; not in tables of stone, but in the fleshy tables of the heart."

II Corinthians 3:3

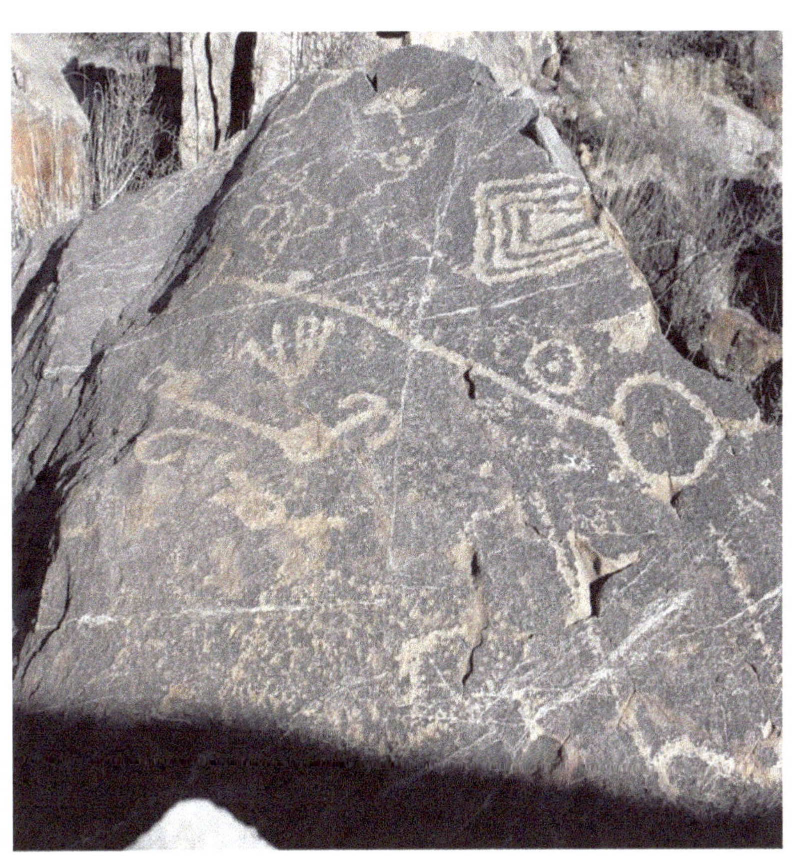

Examine the pictographs closely.
Use your imagination.
Note when an object is near a crack.
Look at the direction which it is headed.
Is it standing still or walking? Hmmm…

———————————————

"And He gave unto Moses, when He had made an end of communing with him upon mount Sinai, two tables of testimony, tables of stone, written with the finger of God."

Exodus 31:18

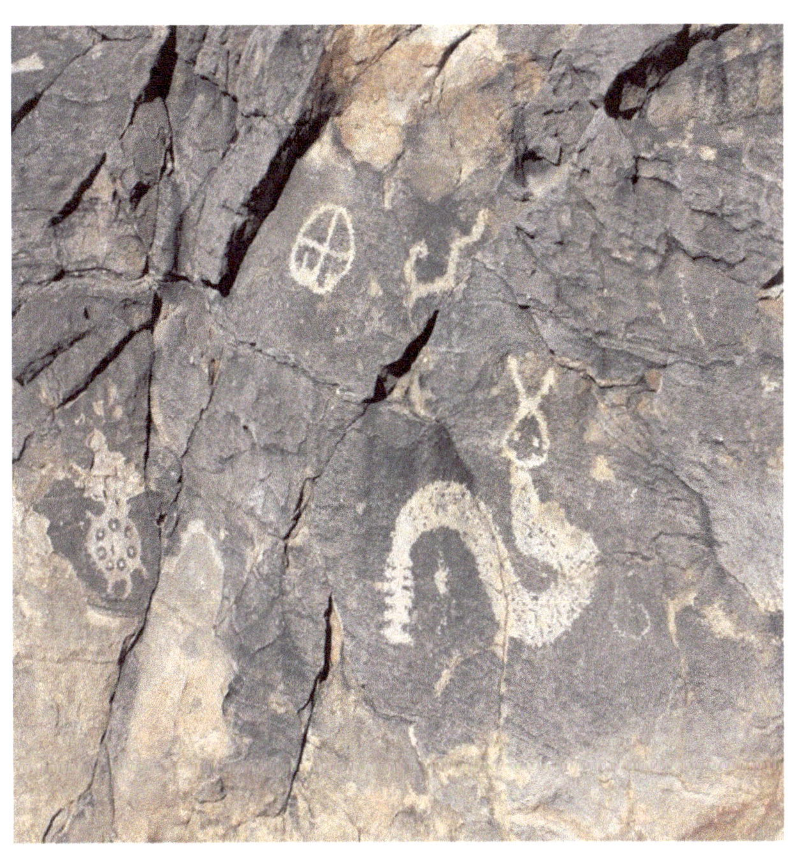

Note, the two sheep; both are walking forward but they are headed in opposite directions! And look at their tails; they are curled up, meaning they are making a round trip. This is a big story!

---

"Gather the people together, men, and women, and children, and thy stranger that is within thy gates, that they may hear, and that they may learn, and fear the Lord your God, and observe to do all the words of this law"

Deuteronomy 31:12

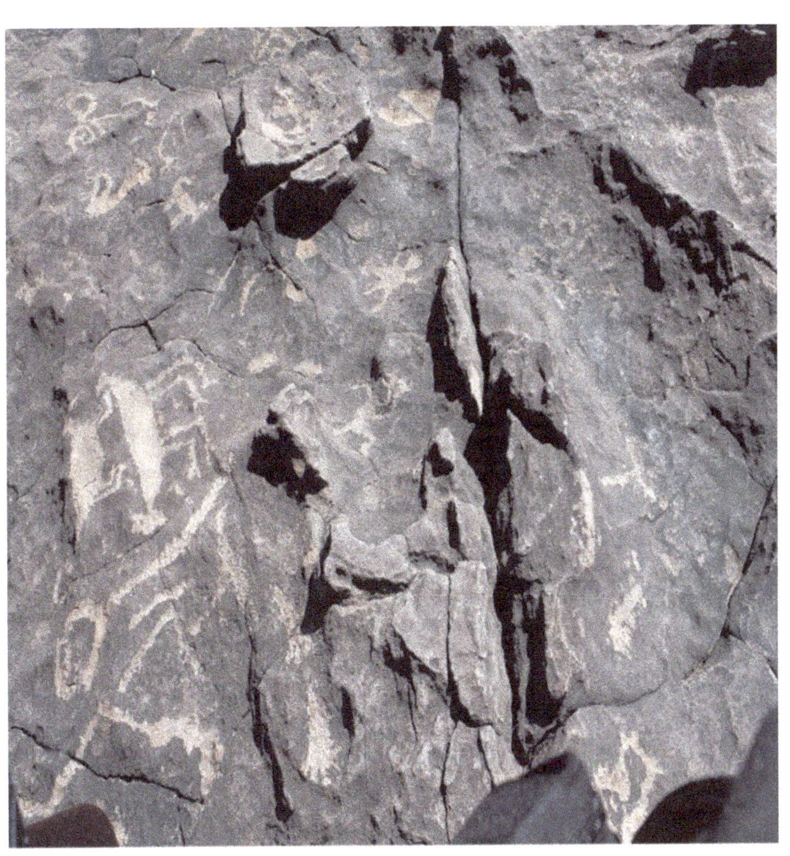

# The more I look at these pictures, the more we can see in them.
# Try to figure out this one…

---

"Behold, I shew you a mystery; We shall not all sleep, but we shall all be changed."

I Corinthians 15:51

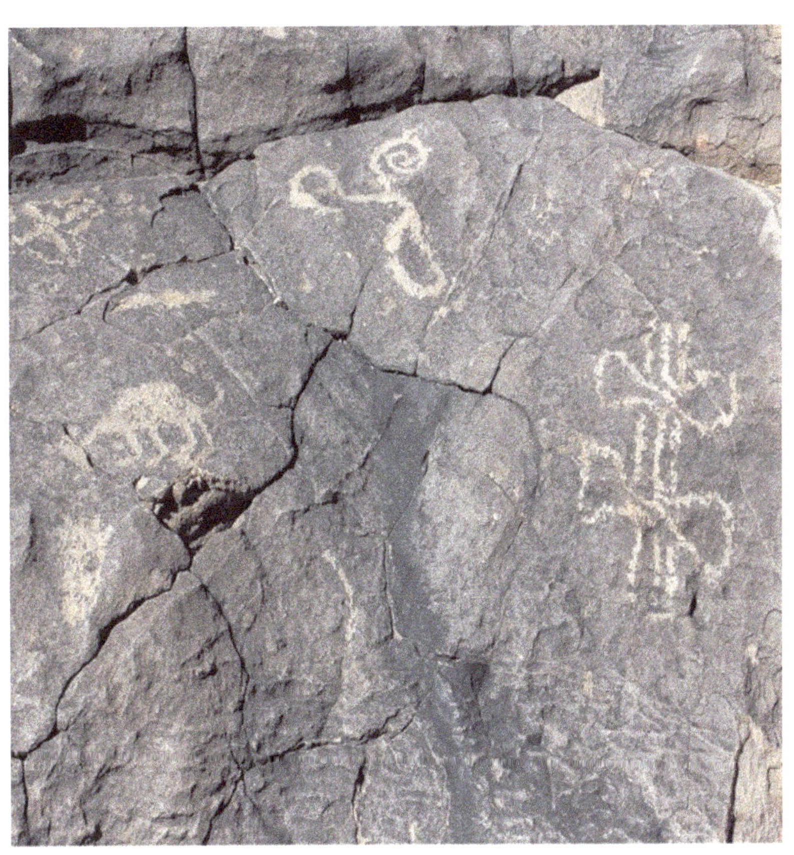

These are still in Pony Hills, but they are a little more difficult to find. They also are telling a different story, so probably a different group made these.

---

"Behold, I will send my messenger, and he shall prepare the way before me…"

Malachi 3:1

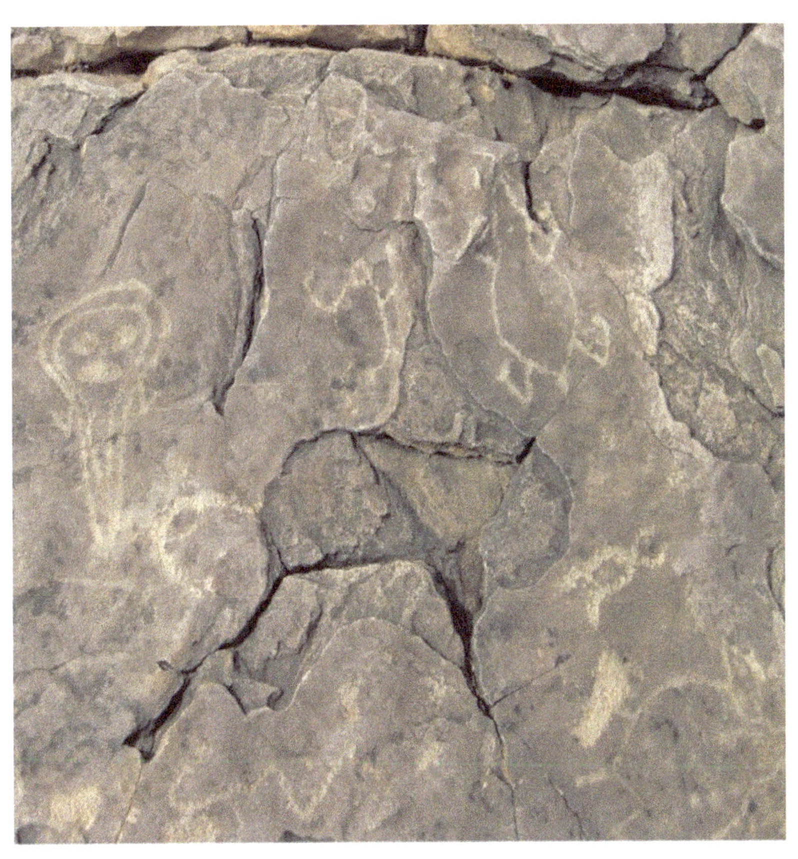

This is my favorite one; Kokopelli is known for bringing seed to the people so that they have a good harvest.
The hump on his back is the bag of seeds that he is carrying.

---

"He that goeth forth and weepeth, bearing Precious seed, shall doubtless come again with rejoicing, bringing his sheaves with him."

Psalm 126:6

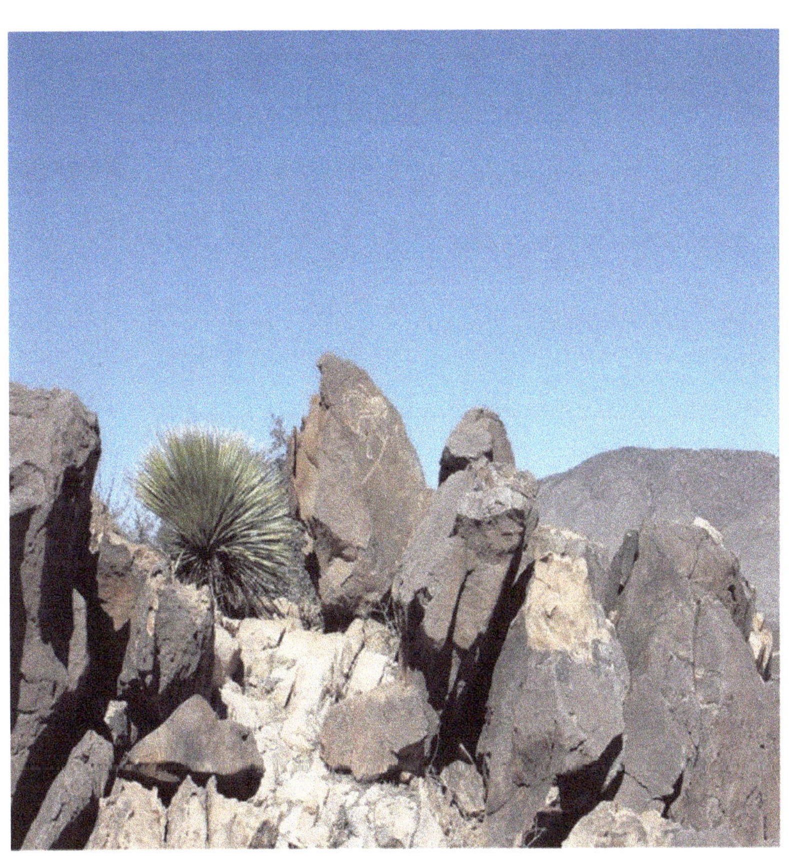

It is always good to have some fun,
so here are some ants having great fun by
playing some music.

---

"Behold their sitting down, and their rising up; I am their music."

Lamentations 4:63

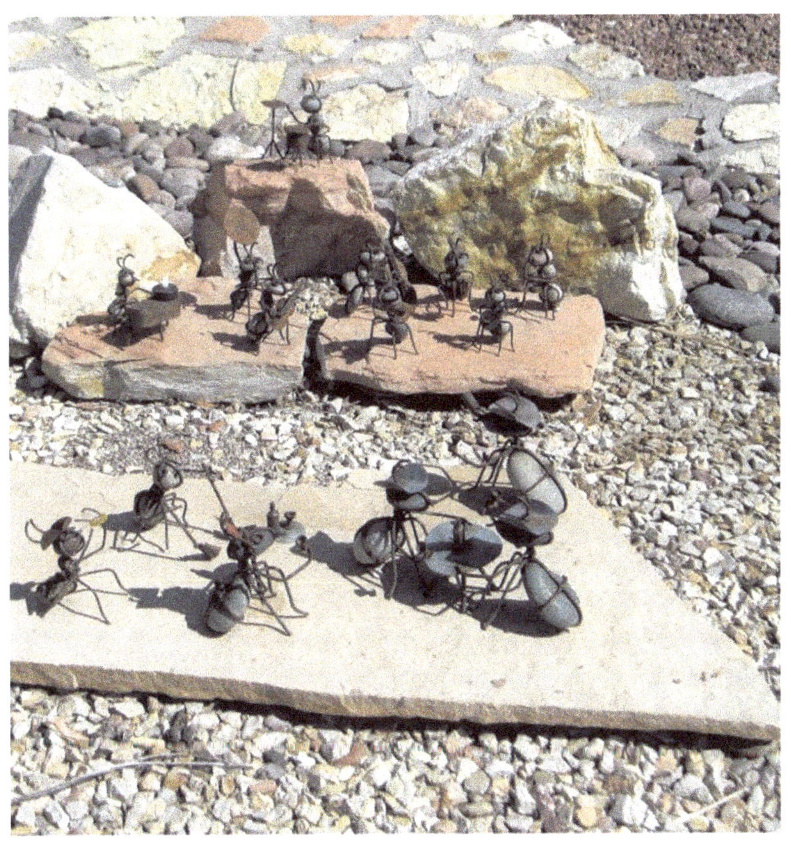

# When you are finished with your music, head over to the playground, and have lots more fun and exercise!

---

"For bodily exercise profiteth little: but godliness is profitable unto all things…"

I Timothy 4:8

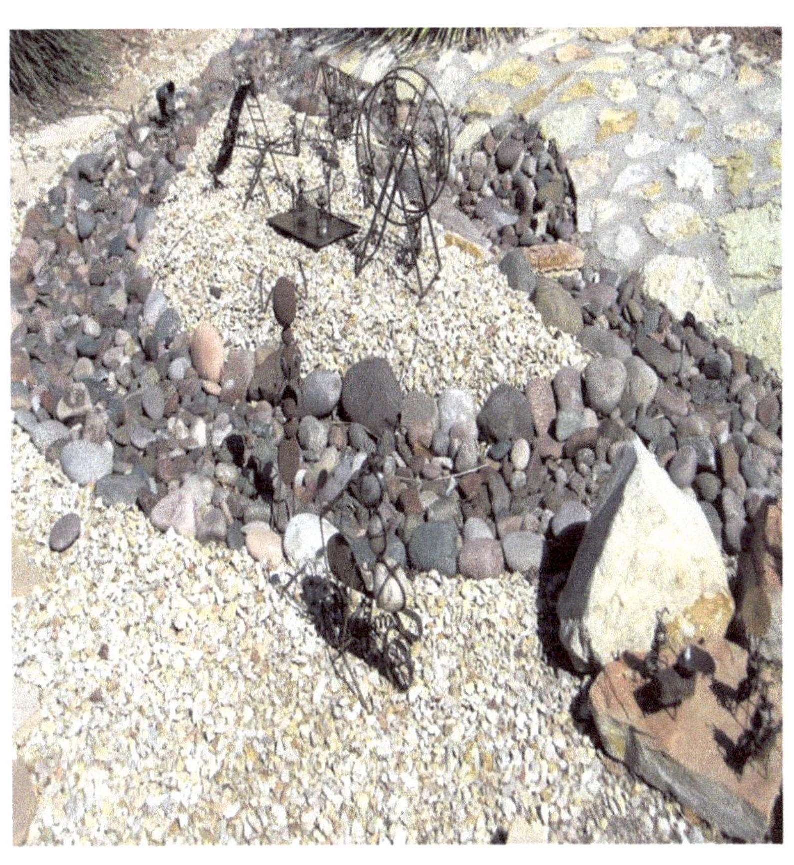

Stand back and look at this one from a distance. Here is where fun comes in while doing photography; a great S-curve.

---

"For the king knoweth of these things, before whom also I speak freely; for I am persuaded that none of these things are hidden from Him; for this thing was not done in a corner."

Acts 26:26

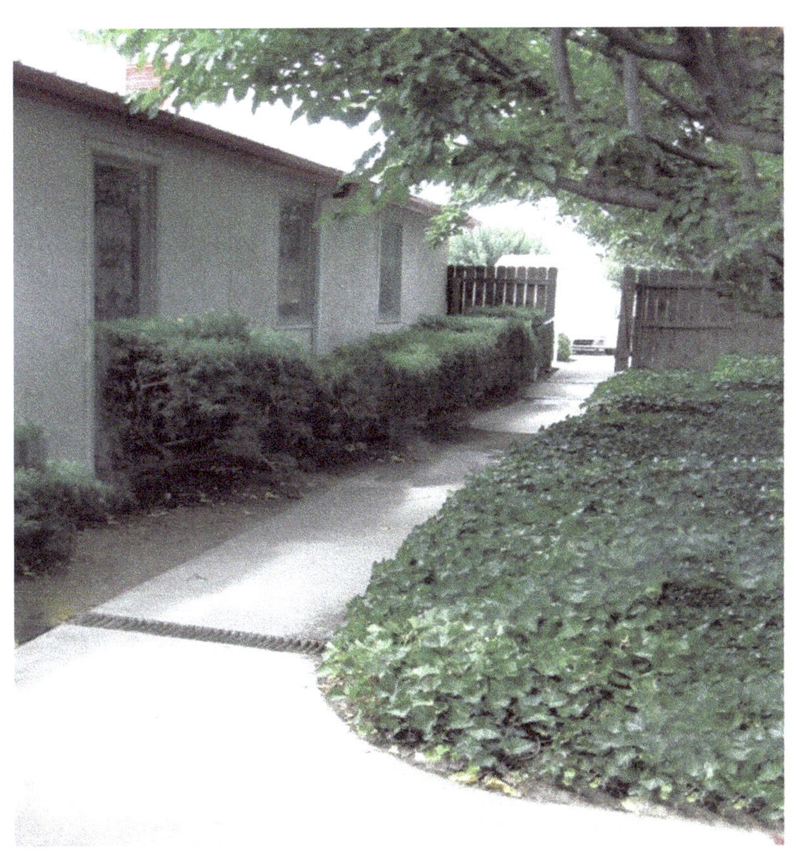

# And now we come to the great New Mexico Sunset! This is over Red Mountain way off in the distance.

---

"Teach me, O Lord, the way of Thy statutes; and I shall keep it unto the end."

Psalm 119:33

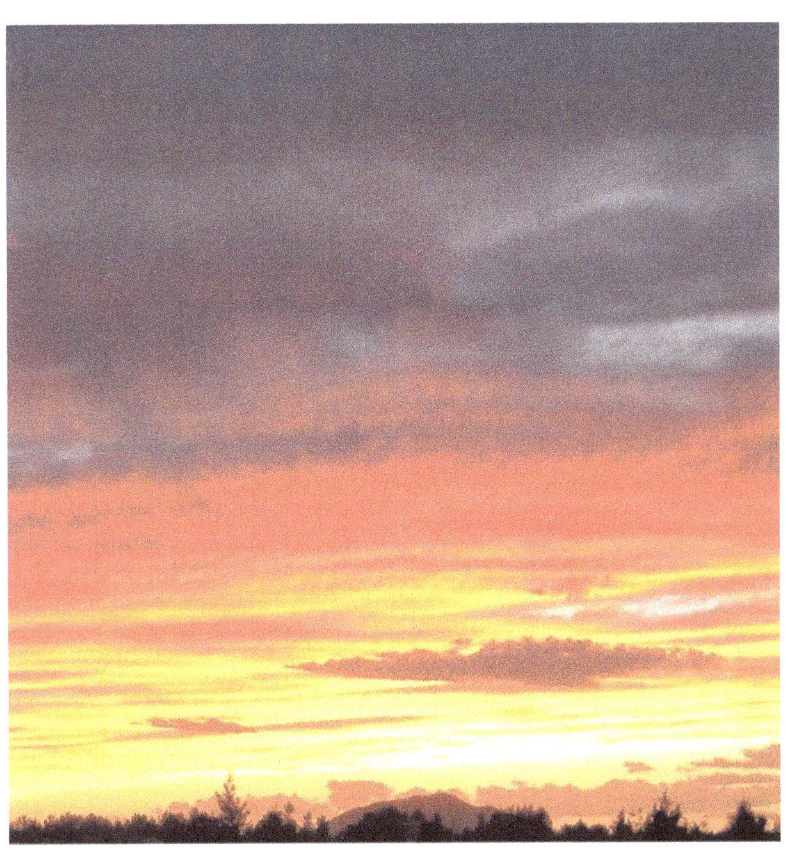

*THE
END*